WILD Animals

EXPLORE

THE FASCINATING WORLDS OF . . .

PANDAS
by Kathy Feeney

CHEETAHS
by Winnie MacPherson

ELEPHANTS
by Anthony D. Fredericks

KOALAS
by Kathy Feeney

Illustrations by John F. McGee

NORTHWORD PRESS
Minnetonka, Minnesota

© NorthWord Press, 2000

Photography ©: Mike Barlow/Dembinsky Photo Associates: 90; Erwin & Peggy Bauer: cover-koala, 51, 74, 86-87, 143, 152, 155, 156, 160, 166-167, 170, 185; Craig Brandt: 55; John Cancalosi/Tom Stack & Associates: 179; W. Perry Conway/Tom Stack & Associates: 112-113; Digital Stock: cover-sunset sky; Adam Jones/Dembinsky Photo Associates: 50, 62; Ed Kanze/Dembinsky Photo Associates: 142, 169; Stephen J. Krasemann: cover-cheetah; Tom & Pat Leeson: cover-panda, 4, 5, 8-9, 10, 12, 15, 16, 18-19, 22, 24-25, 29, 30-31, 33, 35, 43, 44-45, 46, 96, 104-105, 114, 118, 125, 128-129, 132, 134, 137, 141; Joe McDonald/Tom Stack & Associates: cover-elephants, 97, 117, 138-139; Stan Osolinski/Dembinsky Photo Associates: 107, 126; Brian Parker/Tom Stack & Associates: 163; Fritz Polking/Dembinsky Photo Associates: 56, 61, 70, 72-73, 78, 82, 88, 93; Len Rue, Jr.: 58-59, 76-77; John Shaw: 147, 151, 173, 182; John Shaw/Tom Stack & Associates: 120-121; Inga Spence/Tom Stack & Associates: 159, 164, 176; Mark J. Thomas/Dembinsky Photo Associates: 95, 110-111; Roy Toft/Tom Stack & Associates: 122-123; Dave Watts/Tom Stack & Associates: 174, 180; Pan Wenshi/National Geographic Image Collection: 38-39; Martin Withers/Dembinsky Photo Associates: 148; Art Wolfe: 64, 66-67, 69, 98-99, 108, 130-131, 186; Lu Zhi/National Geographic Image Collection: 36-37.

Illustrations by John F. McGee

NorthWord Press
5900 Green Oak Drive
Minnetonka, MN 55343
1-800-328-3895

Library of Congress Cataloging-in-Publication Data

Wild animals : explore the fascinating worlds of -- / illustrations by John F. McGee.
    p. cm.
   Contents: Pandas / by Kathy Feeney -- Cheetahs / by Winnie MacPherson -- Elephants / by Anthony D. Fredericks -- Koalas / by Kathy Feeney.
   Summary: Describes the habitat, appearance, food, and behavior of four threatened or endangered animals.
   ISBN 1-55971-726-2 (hardcover) — ISBN 1-55971-741-6 (pbk.)
   1. Giant panda -- Juvenile literature. 2. Cheetah -- Juvenile literature.
3. Elephants -- Juvenile literature. 4. Koala -- Juvenile literature. [1. Endangered species.]
I. McGee, John F., ill. II. Feeney, Kathy. III. MacPherson, Winnie, Cheetahs for kids.
IV. Fredericks, Anthony D. Elephants for kids.

   QL706.2.W58 1999
   599—dc21   99-047731

Printed in Malaysia

10   9   8   7   6   5   4   3   2

WILD Animals

TABLE OF CONTENTS

Pandas for Kids

by Kathy Feeney
photography by Tom and Pat Leeson
illustrated by John F. McGee

All of the photographs in this book are of giant pandas unless noted.

One summer I saw a panda. A real one, not a stuffed animal in a toy store. Real pandas are from China. That is where Grandfather grew up.

My name is May, and I'm 10 years old, going on 11.

I have always loved pandas. When I was little, Grandfather gave me a toy panda for my birthday. And then one summer he took me to a zoo to see two visiting pandas.

They were awesome! I saw one somersault across the grass. The other one went splashing through a waterfall. Someday I hope to travel to China with Grandfather and see a panda in the wild.

The panda is a symbol for China, like the bald eagle is for the United States. China lends pandas to a few zoos around the world. They share pandas so people can learn about them by seeing them.

Not everyone can see one, even if you live in China. When Grandfather was a boy, many pandas wandered the dense bamboo forests near his village. Now they are very rare.

Scientists think there could be fewer than 1,000 pandas left in the wild.

The giant panda is an endangered species.

Pandas are an endangered species, which means that they might one day become extinct. But it also means that there is still time to save them.

Grandfather's brother, Uncle Lee, is a biologist. He works at a research station in a place called a panda reserve.

The Chinese government creates reserves to protect the panda. Like an oasis in the desert, a research station is a sanctuary within the panda's natural habitat.

Scientists also take pandas to research stations if they become sick or injured.

Resting on a log, this panda is at home in the remote misty mountains of China.

When Grandfather
came to live with
my parents and me,
he told us many
panda stories. He also
read his letters from
Uncle Lee to us.

Grandfather said
I would find out even
more about pandas
if I wrote to Uncle Lee
myself. I thought I knew
everything about pandas.

Then Uncle Lee
and I became pen pals.
Every time I get a
letter from Uncle Lee,
I learn something new.

*The shy and gentle panda likes
to live alone.*

Some ancestors of the panda lived about 3 million years ago in Asia, in places we now call Burma, Laos, Vietnam and China. Today pandas are found only in the mountains of China.

Their real name is giant panda. Their Chinese name is daxiong mao (that's pronounced dah-shwing MA-hoo).

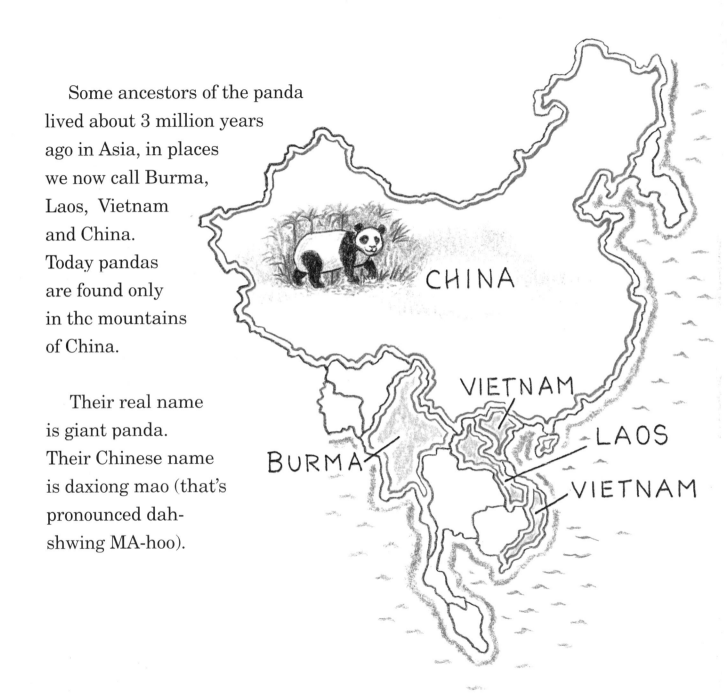

CHINA

VIETNAM

LAOS

VIETNAM

BURMA

Most people just call them pandas. Even though "giant" is part of their name, pandas aren't really that big. It would take about 50 pandas to weigh as much as one elephant.

But they do have a giant white face with black patches around dark brown eyes. Pandas have a black nose, white whiskers and a pink tongue. And round black ears that wiggle when they chew bamboo.

This panda munches a stalk of bamboo. Bamboo is 99 percent of the panda's diet.

Pandas are plump with short strong legs and stubby white tails. They walk "pigeon-toed," with their front feet turned inward. Lumbering through the misty mountains with their heads held low, pandas appear slow and clumsy.

"However, they are quite coordinated," wrote Uncle Lee. "Pandas are great climbers with amazing balance. They trot like horses when they're startled. And they even swim through mountain streams."

Some scientists believe the panda's black-and-white coat helps it blend into the shadowy bamboo forests.

17

Pandas climb trees when they need a safe place to hide or sleep, but they spend most of their time walking the forest floor.

They have natural snowshoes for feet. The pads of their paws are covered with fur, making it easy for them to walk on snowy slopes and icy rocks in winter.

Grandfather believes pandas are so popular because they're so peaceful. Some people say they're popular because they are so rare. I think it's because they look so soft and gentle.

The panda's thick and stiff fur is like a waterproof coat, protecting it from rain and snow.

"They may seem soft," said Grandfather. "But panda fur is really rough."

Touching a panda would feel like petting a dog with a bristly coat.

"Unlike dogs and children, pandas get clean by rolling in dirt!" said Grandfather. "They then comb the dirt out of their coats with their claws and wash up by licking their fur."

Uncle Lee sent me a drawing of a panda. It shows that the skin underneath the panda's coat is two different colors. Under the white fur is pink skin. Beneath the black fur is dark skin.

Some biologists say their color combination helps pandas blend into the shadowy forests to avoid danger.

Pandas have excellent senses of smell and hearing. Scientists have trouble tracking them because pandas hide when they smell and hear humans coming. Yet pandas have poor eyesight.

"Sometimes they walk right past their food without seeing it," Uncle Lee wrote in one of his letters.

Pandas are shy and gentle. But they have razor sharp claws for grasping bamboo. That's their favorite food. Bamboo is a hollow grass that can grow as thick as a broomstick and as tall as a telephone pole.

A panda eats about 25,000 pounds of bamboo in one year. That's about the weight of 10 big cars!

Pandas pause for a meal wherever they find bamboo. What a messy eater!

Pages 24-25: Pandas often eat lying on their backs, sides or bellies.

Scientists say bamboo is 99 percent of the panda's diet. Pandas need to eat a lot of bamboo because it doesn't give them much nourishment. They also like to snack on fruit, roots, wildflowers, and even birds, fish and eggs.

When Grandfather and Uncle Lee were boys, they saw a panda sneaking honey from a beehive!

Pandas nibble nearly all day and into the night. They spend up to 14 hours a day just eating. Imagine if people woke up in the morning and did nothing but eat until they went to bed.

It's no wonder pandas grow up to 5 feet long and weigh between 200 and 350 pounds.

When they're not munching their way through the bamboo forest, pandas sleep. They nap 2 to 4 hours at a time, sprawled either on their sides, backs or bellies. Sometimes pandas snore while they snooze, just like Grandfather in his favorite chair!

Some people call them panda bears. "But a panda may not be a bear at all," wrote Uncle Lee. "Nobody really knows what they are. Some scientists think pandas are related to bears because they look so much alike. Both have round heads, fat bodies and thick fur."

Pandas sometimes snack on wildflowers.

But there are also some differences between the two. For instance, pandas don't hibernate like some bears do. And their teeth are different. Like most bears, pandas have 42 teeth. But a panda's wide back teeth are powerful and very large—perfect for crushing and grinding bamboo.

There is another panda in China, called the lesser or red panda. Most scientists agree that the red panda is probably related to the raccoon.

It is about the size of a large cat. The red panda has a fox-like face with pointed ears, soft reddish brown fur and a long bushy tail.

Red pandas also love bamboo, but eat only the leaves and stems. They cannot eat the woody stalks.

The red panda shares part of the giant panda's name, but it is a closer cousin to raccoons than to bears.

Giant pandas have five fingers on each of their front paws. They also have a special "thumb." They use their thumbs to grab and hold bamboo. They usually eat sitting up, with their legs stretched out straight in front of them. Grasping bamboo stalks with their front paws, they use their fingers and thumbs to peel away the tough outer layers before eating the tender centers.

Pandas are solitary, which means they like to be by themselves. Pandas live with each other only when they are ready to mate or when a mother is raising her cub.

Pandas roam the forests searching for bamboo, so they may sleep in a different place each night.

But pandas are never really alone. They create silent messages for each other by clawing the trunks of trees. The scratched-off bark says: "I'm a panda, and I've been here."

Giant pandas are shy and normally quiet. When they do talk, pandas bark, bleat, chirp, growl, honk, roar, snort, squeal or yip.

Uncle Lee has learned the meaning of each sound.

"Pandas in danger bark like dogs," he wrote. "When they are afraid, they squeal like pigs. During courtship, the males roar like bears."

A panda's daily search for bamboo keeps it wandering through the forest, so it doesn't really have a permanent home.

Pandas have strong jaws and sharp teeth–just what they need to tear apart tough plants.

Males and females get together in the spring to mate. After mating, the male and female go their separate ways. For the next five months, the mother prepares for the birth of her cub. She makes a bed of bamboo twigs and grasses in a cave, a hollow tree or among some rocks.

"Keeping her cub hidden is most important," said Grandfather, "because leopards and wild dogs will prey on baby pandas."

In autumn, mother pandas give birth to one or two babies. A newborn panda is so small it could fit in the palm of a person's hand. Its cry sounds like a human baby. It doesn't even look like a panda. It is pink with fine white fur. By the time the cub is a month old, it has its black-and-white markings.

A newborn panda is smaller than a kitten.

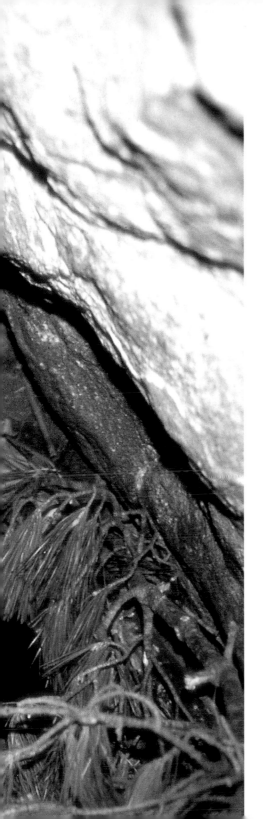

Baby pandas nurse for up to 14 hours a day. When the mother needs to find her own food, she leaves the den, holding the cub close to her chest with one paw while walking on just three legs. As the baby grows, she carries it with her mouth, like a cat.

A cub is born with its eyes closed. It sees for the first time at two months old. By five months, it has stopped nursing and begins to eat soft stalks of bamboo. At one year, a cub weighs around 70 pounds.

When not roaming in search of food, a mother panda and her cub may hide in a cave.

Before its second birthday, a panda is prepared to leave its mother and begin living on its own. Around 4 years old, pandas are mature enough to start families of their own. Scientists say pandas in the wild can live to be about 25 years old.

No matter what age they are, pandas always enjoy playing.

Uncle Lee saw one sledding through the snow. The panda slid down a hill on its belly, climbed back up, and slid all the way back down again!

People outside of China didn't even know about the giant panda until modern times. Americans first saw a panda in 1936.

People are not allowed to capture giant pandas in the wild, and killing one would be a serious crime. The Chinese government protects them. Pandas are thought of as their national treasure.

One threat to the panda is the destruction of bamboo forests. As people cut down trees for logs and build villages farther into the forests, pandas lose their habitat and must travel higher and higher into the mountains for bamboo.

Pandas are excellent climbers, even though they spend most of their time on the ground.

Pages 44-45: From nose to tail, pandas are about 5 feet long.

Uncle Lee and other scientists are working to save the panda.

When they find a panda, the researchers give it a shot so it will fall asleep. The scientists then measure and weigh the panda and check its teeth to find out its age. Before it is released, they attach a radio collar around its neck. By listening to a special machine that receives beeps from the collar, they can follow the panda through the forest and learn more about how it lives.

Just as I was daydreaming about how much fun it would be to study a panda in the wild, Grandfather called to me.

"Special delivery for May!"

It was a package from China. It was larger than Uncle Lee's other letters and was labeled **PHOTOGRAPH: DO NOT BEND!**

The panda is one of the most popular animals in the world.

Grandfather watched while I opened it. Inside was a big picture of Uncle Lee kneeling beside a young giant panda. The panda was wearing a radio collar.

"We are ready to release this panda back into the wild," Uncle Lee wrote. "Perhaps you can help us track her when you come to visit me in China one day. We call this panda something very special."

Her name is May!

Cheetahs for Kids

Cheetahs often help clean each other.

by *Winnie MacPherson*
illustrated by *John F. McGee*

AFRICA

Serengeti

After traveling many miles on trains, boats and airplanes, we finally arrived in Africa. My name is Beth and I am 11 years old. My parents are wildlife photographers. We are always visiting interesting and exciting places so they can take pictures.

For the first time, we were on the plains of the Serengeti in Africa, to photograph cheetahs. The Serengeti is a wildlife refuge covering thousands of square miles in eastern Africa.

Cheetahs live on this open grassland, where they find their favorite prey such as gazelles and impalas. Sometimes, they also hunt hares. Those animals live here because they like to eat the grass and small plants that grow here on the Serengeti.

On the first day of our trip, I awoke before dawn.
I was much too excited to fall back asleep. It was time
to get up if I was going to see some cheetahs. They
usually move about to hunt for food early in the
morning, before the sun is too hot.

After breakfast, I helped my dad put the cameras
in the truck. Our guide knew a lot about cheetahs
and took us to places where they could be observed.
Using my binoculars, I saw many unusual animals.
I couldn't wait to see a real cheetah!

As we rode along, I thought about some of the
things I knew about cheetahs. They belong to the cat
family, whose members are called felids (FE-lidz).

Cheetah cubs stay near their mother for protection.

Cheetahs often climb trees to play, to look around and to leave scent marks. But cheetahs never climb trees to hide their prey in the branches, as leopards do. Cheetahs outrun their prey on the open plains, instead of pouncing on it from a hiding place, as lions and leopards do.

Cheetahs may seem to be flying as they chase their prey.

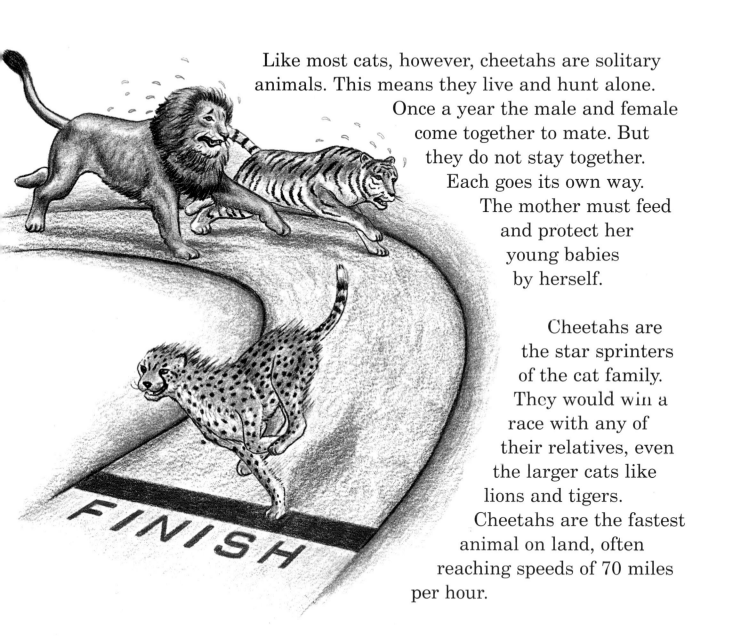

Like most cats, however, cheetahs are solitary animals. This means they live and hunt alone. Once a year the male and female come together to mate. But they do not stay together. Each goes its own way. The mother must feed and protect her young babies by herself.

Cheetahs are the star sprinters of the cat family. They would win a race with any of their relatives, even the larger cats like lions and tigers. Cheetahs are the fastest animal on land, often reaching speeds of 70 miles per hour.

Pages 58-59: Cheetahs like to be high to better see around them.

We had driven about 20 minutes when, suddenly, I saw a family of cheetahs. A female cheetah was sitting on top of a large termite mound. Her three young, called cubs, were sitting with her.

Cheetahs like to sit on the high mounds so they can watch what is going on around them. It is a good way to look for prey and for enemies.

When we drove closer, the mother came down from the top of the mound and stood watching us. Cheetahs are really shy animals. This mother was cautious about anything coming too close to her cubs.

Cubs must learn to be still and watchful.

The mother was beautiful. She was standing tall and proud. Her short, golden fur was covered with black spots. In fact, the name cheetah means "spotted one." The spots on her tail made rings toward the fluffy tip, which was white. Her belly was also white.

Because she had such a large chest and large thigh muscles, her waist looked extra small. She had long, thin legs. They looked very strong. Her feet were thin too, not rounded like other cats' feet.

Her head was rounded on top and seemed very small. Cheetahs have a brow that sticks out over their sharp-sighted eyes. This helps protect their eyes from the sun. In very bright light, the pupils of their golden eyes become small dots.

The Serengeti grasses are good camouflage.

Like other members of the cat family, cheetahs have excellent eyesight.

Two black stripes ran down the female's face. They started from the inner corner of each eye and went around the outside of her mouth. Some scientists call these stripes "tear lines," since they run down a cheetah's face like tears. These lines and their spots are good camouflage (KAM-uh-flaj) for the cheetah when it hides in the grass. They help cheetahs get very close to prey without being seen.

The female's small, round ears were low on her
head. Her hearing is so keen she may hear prey before
she sees it. And when she hears a sound, she doesn't
have to turn her head as humans do to find out where
it came from. She just moves her ears.

The cubs had the same color and markings as their mother—except that their bodies were covered with a layer of long, smoke-gray fur. It was like the fluff on a baby bird. This fur was even longer on their shoulders and down their back.

They will lose this gray fur when they are about 3 months old. Then their coat will be golden like their mother's.

Cubs don't hurt each other when they play-fight.

67

We guessed that the cubs were about 6 weeks old. During the first six weeks of their life, cubs stay in their lair under a bush. The female cheetah has to leave them alone when she goes hunting.

This might have been the cubs' first day out on the plains with their mother. These cheetah cubs were born before the spring rainy season had turned the grass green. I could see that their baby fur blended with the dry grass. It helped to hide the cubs.

The female had brought the cubs with her so they would be closer to their food. Before she could hunt, though, she had to find a new safe lair where the cubs could rest.

As the fluffy cub grows, its fur will become sleek.

The cubs would not be able to help their mother hunt yet. In fact, they might make trouble for her. Such young cubs often accidentally warn the prey with their whimpering and playing in the grass. From 6 to 12 months old, the cubs follow their mother to learn her skills when she hunts. They will not hunt large prey on their own until they are about 12 to 16 months old.

Sometimes cubs want to play when they should be learning to hunt.

The largest of the cubs became curious and slowly moved down from the mound. It stood near its mother and stared at me. Suddenly, the cub wrinkled its face and spat.

This startled me and made me jump. But I couldn't help laughing. The cub was so small, and it tried so hard to be ferocious.

Soon the female decided that we were not going to harm them. She made a chirping sound, and the other two cubs came to her.

The cheetah family slowly moved away from us across the plains. The female cheetah's sharp eyes kept watching for prey to catch for dinner. She must hunt every day to feed herself and her cubs. Cheetahs can live for 5 or more days without water, if they have meat to eat.

Newborn cheetahs get all their food from their mother.

Shade from a tree is a good place for a cheetah to rest.

We followed them while Mom and Dad took pictures. Finally, they turned and disappeared into the tall grass. All we could see was the white tip of the female's tail. It is this white tip of their mother's tail that the cubs follow when going through high grass. I watched it too, until they were out of sight.

The hot sun was burning my face. We decided it was time to return to our camp and the shade of the trees. The cheetahs were leaving the open plains for the shelter of their bushes.

The next day, we returned to the same place, hoping to see the female with her cubs again. A hot wind blew across the plains.

On our way, we passed some young male cheetahs roaming across the grass together. Sometimes, after leaving their mother, young cheetah brothers live and hunt together. These groups of young males are called coalitions (ko-uh-LISH-unz). They hunt and protect their small territory of about 15 square miles.

Group hunting is often more successful than hunting alone.

All at once we saw a female cheetah. She was growling, and she kept looking nervously at a nearby large clump of bushes.

Suddenly we saw four female lions running toward the bush.

"I know what's worrying her," Dad said. "She has cubs hidden in the bush. If the lions find her cubs, they will kill them. The cheetah cannot go near the bush or she will reveal the cubs' hiding place."

It was clear the lions were searching for something. I was sure they had scented (SENT-ed), or smelled, the cheetah cubs. Then I realized they weren't even looking at the bush. They ran right past it. The cubs were safe!

Cubs must stay alert when they are hiding from danger.

As soon as the lions were gone, the female cheetah ran to the bush and called her cubs to her. She used the same chirping sound we had heard the day before.

Cheetahs also make many other sounds like squeals, yelps and purrs. Some are used for teaching the cubs. Some are used for warning of danger. Some are used when they are contented.

Females often purr loudly while washing or feeding their cubs. Male cheetahs, however, do not roar, as lions do.

Mother cheetahs are very patient with their playful cubs.

On the tenth day of our trip, we found our cheetah family again. The female was sitting on the same termite mound. One of the cubs was sitting between her front legs. I saw the other two playing at the bottom of the mound.

One cub hid in the grass and leaped out at the other when it passed. Then they rolled together in the grass, over and over. They took turns hiding and pouncing.

Sometimes they gave each other little nips on the back or neck. When cubs run and play-fight they are really practicing for when they grow up and have to hunt and defend themselves.

Soon the mother cheetah and the third cub joined in the game of hide-and-pounce. She was enjoying the game as much as the cubs. It was fun watching them play.

At one time, all four of the cheetahs were chasing each other in a circle. The mother and cubs played together for quite a while. She was very patient, even when they tugged on her tail and jumped at her face.

Suddenly, the female stopped and began watching a nearby herd of impalas eating leaves from bushes. The impalas did not see the cheetahs. Giving her cubs the signal to hide, she slowly crouched low to the ground. The cubs ran under a bush.

Silently, the mother cheetah moved through the thin grass toward the impalas. She never stopped watching them. If she felt the impalas had seen her, she crouched and stayed perfectly still.

Her sneaky walk quickened to a run. Suddenly, she was in a super sprint!

Cheetahs have good balance, even when running at top speed.

The dry dust from the plains flew up in a cloud behind her. When the impalas saw the cheetah racing toward them, they rushed away in a stampede.

Impalas keep an eye on nearby cheetahs at all times.

Cheetahs are built for running at high speed. Everything about them is light and sleek. In fact, an adult cheetah only weighs about 100 to 130 pounds. Some lions weigh as much as 500 pounds.

Cheetahs have slender bodies and small heads. Their narrow, sharp teeth fit together in their jaw, and work like scissor blades. There is no space for the large front teeth other cats have.

Their whiskers are short and not very thick. Since they hunt in the grass during the day, they don't need long whiskers to help them find their way through thick, dark bushes.

A big yawn shows the cheetah's sharp teeth.

The claws on a cheetah's small, thin feet are not retractable like those of a house cat. This means they cannot be pulled back into their toes. Because the claws are out all the time, they lose their sharpness and become worn down. But this wearing down makes them thick and strong.

The pads on a cheetah's feet are small and tough. When the cheetah runs, the edges of the pads grip the ground like rubber soles on sneakers. Cheetahs also have strong leg muscles.

The cheetah's limber spine is another key to its speed. It works like a spring. The cheetah curves its back and pulls its feet together. Then, the back uncoils and the long legs fly out as far as they can reach. As soon as the front legs touch the ground again, the spine coils up and gives the legs another powerful push.

Each time the cheetah's back bends and stretches, it gives more power to the legs to reach even farther. The cheetah soars through the air in mighty leaps!

A cheetah's strong feet and short, tough claws tightly grip the ground. Its long, thick tail swings back and forth as the cheetah turns and twists after its prey. The tail helps to keep the cheetah balanced.

While on a chase, the cheetah breathes in huge gulps of air through large nostrils to its large lungs. It may take as many as 150 breaths a minute. This is much faster than its regular breathing.

From standing still, cheetahs can reach a speed of 70 miles per hour in seconds. But cheetahs must catch their prey very quickly, for they cannot continue this high speed for much longer than a minute or two.

As we watched, a few of the impalas waited too long before running away, and they were left behind. The female cheetah caught one of them. At last, she had food for her cubs and herself.

Cheetahs must protect their kill from other predators.

But she could not eat yet. Her powerful race had used up all the strength in her body. And she was overheated. She lay down to rest and cool off.

While the cheetah rests, other predators may come and steal the prey. Hyenas, lions and jackals all steal from cheetahs. So the cheetah must try to hide her prey and rest quickly. She must be very lucky. Any of those predators might also kill the cheetah's cubs.

After about 15 minutes, she had caught her breath. Her heart had slowed to its normal beating. The mother cheetah returned to the cubs' hiding place and showed the cubs the way back to the kill. Finally, the cheetah family was able to eat.

A few days later, we had to leave. My parents had taken all the pictures they needed. I was sad that it was time to end our stay on the Serengeti. I would miss our cheetah family.

Maybe I would see the cheetahs on another visit. I was sure I would never forget them.

Elephants for Kids

Elephants often travel through a river to keep cool.

by Anthony D. Fredericks
illustrated by John F. McGee

All photographs in this book are of African elephants unless noted.

My mother is always telling me that I have a good memory. I can remember what to buy at the grocery store. I can remember the batting averages of all the players on my favorite baseball team. And I can remember lots of things in school, especially in science, which is my favorite subject.

Sometimes my mother tells me that I have a memory like an elephant. I like that, because elephants are my favorite animals.

A group of elephants is called a herd.

KENYA

My name is Kwasi (KWAH-zee), and I'm 10 years old. My family moved to the United States from Kenya when I was very young. Kenya is a country in eastern Africa with large areas of grasslands, tall mountains, and lots of wild animals.

I don't remember a lot about my native country, but my father is always telling me about Kenya and its wild animals. I especially like his stories about elephants.

I've already learned a lot about elephants. For instance, a male is called a bull and a female is called a cow. A baby elephant is called a calf. Also, there are two different species (SPEE-sees), or kinds, of elephants: the African elephant and the Asian elephant.

The African elephant, which lives in central and southern Africa, is the world's largest land animal. A bull elephant can weigh up to 15,000 pounds. That's about as heavy as a school bus. Cows are smaller.

A full-grown African elephant may stand 13 feet high at the shoulder. That's taller than a basketball hoop.

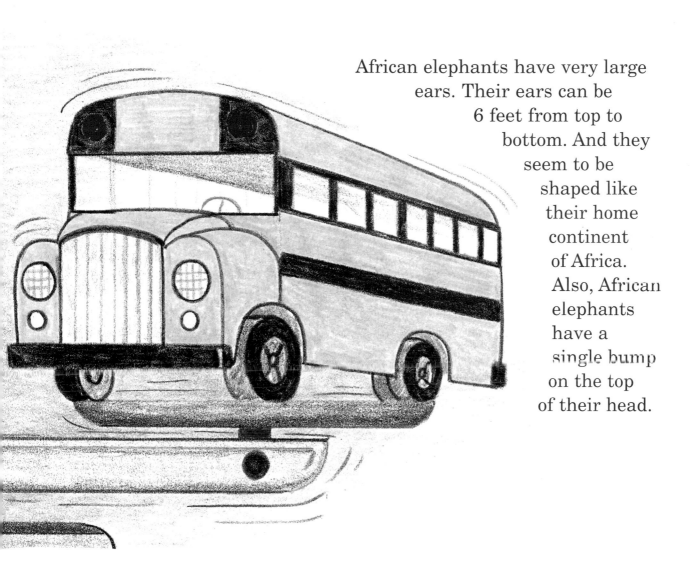

African elephants have very large ears. Their ears can be 6 feet from top to bottom. And they seem to be shaped like their home continent of Africa. Also, African elephants have a single bump on the top of their head.

Pages 104-105: An elephant's hide, or skin, is very tough and its eyes are small.

The Asian elephant, which lives in India and several Southeast Asian countries, is smaller than its African relatives. An adult bull may weigh up to 12,000 pounds and stand about 10 feet tall.

Asian elephants have small ears. Some people say that their ears are shaped like the country of India. Asian elephants have two bumps on the top of their head.

An elephant's eyes are slightly larger than an adult human's eyes. Some people think that because an elephant's eyes are small for its size that it must have poor eyesight. But an elephant can see pretty well, even in the shaded forest. And it can see moving objects up to 150 feet away in bright sunlight.

*The size and shape of the ears on this cow and calf
tell you they are Asian elephants.*

Elephants walk at an average speed of about 5 miles per hour. Even though they are very large animals, they can run at speeds of about 35 miles per hour for short distances.

When elephants are moving quickly across dry savannas, they make a lot of dust.

Many people are surprised to learn that elephants walk on their tiptoes! The weight of an elephant rests on the tip of each toe and on thick pads behind the toes. Elephants are able to walk very quietly through the forest or across the savanna.

Elephants usually live together in two different types of herds. Adult bulls spend most of their time alone or with other bulls. Cows and calves live in their own herds, separate from the males except at mating time.

Cow and calf herds are always led by an older female, known as the matriarch (MAY-tree-ark). She is responsible for the safety of the herd and for helping them find water and food. Since the matriarch may live to be 60 or 70 years old, she may be the leader of a herd for many years.

This cow carefully watches over two calves.

Pages 112-113: Herds of cows and calves stay close as they travel across the hot savanna.

Elephants are very intelligent—and they really do have good memories. The matriarch is able to remember many migration paths, the location of watering holes, and where food can be found.

During the dry season, elephants may travel up to 30 miles in a day looking for food and water. Because she is older and has traveled more, the matriarch may have the best memory of all the elephants in a herd.

You can tell how deep this elephant went into the water by the wet line on its belly.

The first thing most people notice about an elephant is its trunk. An elephant's trunk is made of the nose, upper lip, and muscles of the elephant's face. In fact, an elephant's trunk has nearly 150,000 muscles, but no bones. It's one of the most amazing organs in the animal world.

Elephants sometimes greet each other by wrapping their trunks together. It's almost like a handshake! Elephants also use their trunks to draw up water for drinking or to spray over themselves in hot weather.

An adult elephant can suck up to 12 quarts of water into its trunk at one time and then squirt it into its mouth. During the dry season, elephants can put their trunks down their throats and take water out of their stomach. They spray this water over themselves to cool off.

Elephants use their trunks to wipe their eyes when something gets in them. They sometimes use them to wrestle. Trunks are also good "sniffers."

How would you like to be able to pick things up with your nose? That's what elephants do. They can use their trunks to pick up objects as small as a berry or a single blade of grass. An elephant's trunk can also lift heavy objects, such as logs weighing up to 600 pounds. That's like lifting me and seven of my friends all together!

African elephants have long trunks (up to 8 feet long), with two "fingers" at the tip. Asian elephants have shorter trunks with one triangular "finger." Using its trunk, an elephant can pick fruit, leaves, and branches from a tree up to a height of 20 feet. That's higher than a giraffe can reach!

Elephants must have good balance to be able to stretch for food like this.

Because elephants use their trunks to do so many things, it can take a calf 5 to 6 months to learn how to use its trunk. And when this "tool" gets tired, adult elephants often rest their trunks on the ends of their tusks.

An elephant's tusks are very long teeth, called incisors (in-SIZ-orz), that grow out from the upper jaw. They are made of ivory, which is similar to bone. Humans have incisors too, but they don't grow as long!

These young bulls are play-fighting with each other.

121

Both male and female
African elephants have tusks.
But most Asian females and
many Asian males do not
have tusks, or they are very
short and not seen outside
the jaw. (Scientists aren't
sure why some elephants
don't have tusks.) Tusks of
both species continue to grow
throughout an elephant's
life at a rate of about 4 to 7
inches each year.

*Many Asian elephants like this one
have no tusks.*

Elephants use their tusks for many things. They use them as tools to dig into the ground when looking for water. They use them as weapons—especially the males, which often fight with each other to protect their territories. Elephants also use their tusks as a sign of strength and superiority.

The world record weight for a single African elephant tusk is 259 pounds. The longest tusk on record measured 11 feet 6 inches. That's higher than the ceiling in my classroom at school!

When one elephant moves quickly toward another during a fight, it is called charging.

Just as people are right-handed or left-handed, elephants are right-tusked or left-tusked. If you look closely at an elephant's tusks you will notice that one of them is worn down more than the other. The one that shows the most wear is the one the elephant uses most of the time.

Another interesting thing about an elephant is its tail. An elephant's tail can be as long as 60 inches. The tail hairs on the end may be another 30 inches long. And the tips of the tail hairs often reach the ground.

An elephant's tail is used mostly to keep flies and other insects away. But it can also show an elephant's emotions, or feelings. When an elephant is frightened or angry it will hold its tail high in the air.

You can tell by the length of the tusks that this is a right-tusked elephant.

An elephant uses its ears to help keep cool. In hot weather, an elephant flaps its ears to create a cooling breeze. This also cools the blood in the blood vessels in its ears. It's like built-in air conditioning!

Scientists who study animals are called zoologists (zoe-AH-luh-jists). Those who study elephants can identify individual elephants according to the blood vessel patterns in their ears. They are like "fingerprints." No two elephants have the same pattern.

This calf is learning to flap its ears to keep cool while eating.

Elephants also "talk" with their ears. The matriarch makes her ears stick out to signal members of the herd when there is danger nearby. She also moves her ears to tell them it's time to eat, rest, or travel.

Family members often greet one another by flapping their ears. When the whole herd becomes excited, they all flap their ears wildly. What a sight!

An elephant's skin is nearly hairless and very wrinkled.

My father's friend, Dr. Jacobson, has made several trips to the African country of Tanzania (tan-zan-EE-uh) to study how elephants communicate with each other. In her research, Dr. Jacobson learned that elephants use low-frequency sounds, called rumbling.

While humans are unable to hear these sounds, members of an elephant family can keep in touch with one another over distances of up to 6 miles.

Elephants communicate even while taking a mud bath.

They also make other noises that humans *can* hear.
Sometimes they raise their trunks high in the air
and make loud trumpeting sounds. These sounds,
which can be heard over long distances, usually
mean the elephant is angry or upset.

Elephants don't mind going into deep water to find the best food, like these river plants.

Because of their large size, full-grown elephants need to eat between 300 and 400 pounds of food every day. You and I, on the other hand, eat about 2 to 3 pounds of food a day. Eating that much food takes an elephant about 18 hours a day!

Most people eat lots of different kinds of food, like fruits, vegetables, breads, meat, and fish. Elephants, however, are herbivores (HERB-i-vorz). That means they eat only plant foods. Most of their diet is just plain grass. Sometimes they eat leaves and bark from trees. They also eat fruits, branches, and twigs.

In addition to all that food, an adult elephant can drink up to 3 gallons of water at one time or as much as 24 gallons of water in a day. Imagine if we drank that much water. That would be about 384 glasses of water every day!

Elephants also use water to keep cool. They give themselves lots of showers by spraying themselves with water using their trunks. The water cools them just as a shower cools us. Then, when the water on their skin evaporates, it cools them even more—just as evaporating sweat cools us. (Elephants do not have sweat glands in their skin as we do, so they must keep spraying themselves to keep from overheating.)

Elephants may wallow, or roll around, in a mud pit, which also keeps them cool. Elephants often seem to come in different colors, like red, brown, or black. But that's just the color of the mud they play in.

Elephants sometimes use their trunks to throw dust and mud over themselves. This forms a cooling and protective coating on their skins.

My parents sometimes complain about the wrinkles in their skin. But to an elephant, wrinkles are good. Wrinkles help elephants keep cool in hot weather. When an elephant takes a bath, the cracks and crevices in its skin trap moisture. This cooling moisture takes longer to evaporate from the elephant's skin. A wrinkly elephant keeps cooler much longer than one with fewer wrinkles.

This young cow's many wrinkles will help keep her cool after her bath.

But instead of telling my mother how helpful wrinkles can be, I decided to ask her about baby elephants. She told me that a female elephant usually has just 1 calf about every 4 years.

Gestation (jes-TA-shun) is the amount of time between when a male and female mate and the birth of the baby. For elephants, it is the longest in the animal world: 22 months. That means that a mother elephant is pregnant for almost 2 whole years.

A baby elephant weighs between 180 and 350 pounds when it is born. Newborn human babies weigh only about 7 to 10 pounds. Baby elephants grow very quickly. Very often they gain between 25 and 45 pounds in a month!

This tiny baby will begin to learn from many members of the herd.

139

Many females in the herd help teach and protect the growing calves. They are also very caring toward others in their herd. They may stay near a sick elephant for several days, watching over it and bringing it food.

Many people in countries around the world are working hard to protect elephants. Special game preserves and wild animal parks have been set up in some African and Asian countries.

When I grow up I would like to be a zoologist. I would like to visit my homeland of Kenya and help study and take care of the elephants!

Elephants spend a lot of time eating.

Koalas for Kids

Koalas live only in Australia.

by Kathy Feeney
illustrated by John F. McGee

AUSTRALIA

Some people think koalas look like cuddly toy teddy bears with their shiny brown eyes, fluffy round ears, and rubbery black noses. They are often called "koala bears." But koalas are not bears.

These amazing Australian mammals are actually related to the kangaroo. This means the koala is a marsupial (mar-SOO-pee-ul). A female marsupial carries her baby in a pouch on her belly. But unlike the kangaroo, the koala has a pouch that opens from the bottom, like an upside-down pocket.

Australia is the only place on Earth where koalas are found in the wild. Years ago they roamed throughout this island continent. But now koalas live only in the eucalyptus (yoo-kul-IP-tus) tree forests along Australia's eastern and southern coasts.

Koalas are nocturnal, which means they are mostly active at night. That is also when they do most of their feeding. The koala's favorite food is the leaves of eucalyptus trees.

Eucalyptus leaves are spear-shaped and contain mostly water. In the morning these leaves are also covered with dew. Koalas get so much water by just eating them that they rarely take a drink. Yet sometimes they will sip water from streams and rivers that run through their forest homes.

Native Australian people are called aborigines (ab-o-RIJ-uh-nees). When they first saw the koala, the aborigines thought the animal never ever drank water. So they gave it a special name. "Koala" is an aboriginal word meaning "no drink."

Koalas are hardly ever thirsty because they get water from eating eucalyptus leaves.

Koalas grow to be about 2 feet tall and can weigh from 10 to 30 pounds. They have white chins and white chests. They also have white fur on the underside of their forearms. The rest of their coat is either gray or brown.

Their coloring blends in well with the eucalyptus tree bark. The fur of their coat is thicker and longer on the back than on the belly.

This koala easily balances on a branch high in a eucalyptus tree.

Their spotted rump also creates a natural camouflage that helps them hide in the trees. Their ears look fluffy and are covered with long, white hair.

There are 3 species (SPEE-sees), or kinds, of koalas: the Victoria, the New South Wales, and the Queensland.

The Victoria and the New South Wales koalas live in the southern part of Australia where the weather is cool. The Victoria koala is the largest. The New South Wales is the middle size of the three kinds. Both of these southern koalas have thick fur to keep them warm. The color of their coat is brown.

The smallest koala is the Queensland. It is found in Australia's warmer northern region. Because of the warmer temperatures where it lives, it has short-haired fur. Its coat is a light shade of gray.

Koalas may look chubby, but underneath their fluffy fur, they are lean and muscular.

Their fur changes to adapt to the different temperatures in their environment. Woolly waterproof coats keep them warm in cold weather and dry in rain.

When the seasons change and the weather warms, they can shed some of their fur to stay cool. It's like the layers of clothing that skiers wear to stay comfortable on the slopes. If they get too warm, they can simply remove a layer of clothing.

A koala's fur is like a warm raincoat.

Koalas do not have a tail. Their rump is padded fur.

While most people need a pillow to sit on something hard, the koala's built-in "cushion" lets it sit for hours on hard tree branches.

The koala's rump is like having a portable pillow.

Koalas have pear-shaped bodies that provide them with good balance for perching on tree limbs. They are rather short and stubby, but they have long, powerful arms and legs. These give them the strength they need for climbing.

Koalas have great coordination as they leap from branch to branch. Koalas would make great Olympic gymnasts!

A koala has 2 thumbs and 3 fingers on each of its front paws. The extra thumb is a terrific tool for pulling and grasping leaves. Like cats, koalas need claws to climb. Sharp, curved claws on their front paws help them grip the smooth, hard bark of the eucalyptus tree.

Koalas have 5 toes on each of their back paws. Except for their first toe, their back paws also have claws. The first toe works like a thumb to hold onto things. The second and third toes are joined together. Koalas can use these connected toes to scratch an itch or to comb their fur. The fourth and fifth toes on their feet are used for climbing.

Under all that long hair are the koala's ears, which are very good at hearing many sounds.

Climbing is easy for koalas. First they dig their front claws into the bark of the eucalyptus tree for a strong hold. Then they push them-selves upward with their back paws, and grab the tree again with their front claws.

They almost appear to be hopping up the tree. The pads on the bottom of their front and back paws prevent them from slipping and falling.

Sharp claws help koalas hold onto a branch, even a very skinny one.

Koalas must always keep a tight grip. This is important because koalas climb very high into these trees, often 150 feet!

That's like a person taking an elevator ride to the fifteenth floor of a building.

They climb so high for two reasons: to be safe and to have plenty of fresh eucalyptus leaves to eat.

When a koala finds a good feeding place, it stops and throws an arm or a leg around a tree limb. It will then wedge its body in between the leafy eucalyptus branches. What a nice setting for a snack and a snooze!

In fact, koalas often become so comfortable in these temporary tree houses they may fall asleep while still chewing. Koalas have been spotted sound asleep with half-eaten eucalyptus leaves hanging from their mouths.

Don't worry, this sleeping koala won't fall out of the tree.

Unlike people, they can sleep while sitting up in a tree—and not fall out. They like sleeping as much as eating. Koalas can nap curled up in a tight ball or loosely draped over branches with their arms and legs hanging down.

They usually stay in the same tree for several days at a time, because moving to another tree is a big job. They must carefully climb backward and retrace their steps all the way to the ground. Then they carefully scoot over to a nearby tree and climb high to reach their next meal.

Changing trees takes a long time and uses a lot of energy.

Tree-dwelling creatures like the koalas are arboreal (ar-BOR-ee-ul), which means they prefer to live high above the ground. Koalas consume only leaves, grasses, and other plants, meaning they are herbivores.

Koalas prefer one type of food. They just love to eat eucalyptus leaves. Some people have a favorite food—like pizza, for example. But they normally do not eat it at every meal!

A koala consumes about 1-1/2 pounds of eucalyptus leaves each day. That's an awful lot for its size. Like squirrels, koalas can store food in their cheeks to save for later. This comes in handy when they are hungry and want a quick snack.

Koalas also eat the stems and bark of eucalyptus trees.

Eucalyptus trees are also called gum trees. They are evergreens, which means they keep their green leaves year-round.

But that doesn't mean they can grow chewing gum! Eucalyptus "gum" is the sticky sap that oozes through the tree's bark.

Koalas have strong arms and legs because sometimes it's a big stretch to reach the next tree limb.

Koalas also like to nibble on the stems, flowers, and bark of the eucalyptus tree. In addition to furnishing koalas with food, these trees provide protection from rain, and shade them from the hot Australian sun.

Eucalyptus leaves are poisonous to most animals. But koalas have special stomachs that can process the tree's oils. Once digested, these strong-scented oils help repel blood-sucking fleas and lice.

The oils also give koalas a sweet eucalyptus scent. Some people say they smell like a refreshing eucalyptus cough drop!

Pages 166-167: The Australian sun can be very hot, so koalas keep cool in the shade of eucalyptus trees.

Koalas have powerful jaws equipped with 30 teeth for chewing. Their scissor-sharp front teeth help them shred the tough eucalyptus leaves. Flat back teeth enable them to grind and mash their meal before swallowing it.

There are about 600 varieties of eucalyptus. But koalas are picky eaters. Scientists estimate that they will only choose to eat between 20 and 30 of them.

Koalas can locate the leaf types they like best just by sniffing the trunks of the eucalyptus trees. The koala's smooth black nose is covered with hundreds of tiny hairs. These special hairs make it especially sensitive to smells.

Once a koala finds a kind of eucalyptus it likes, it will eat and eat and eat.

Like most nocturnal animals, koalas do not have very strong eyesight. They rely more on their superb senses of smell and hearing to warn them of approaching danger. They must be aware of eagles that can swoop down and snatch their babies.

And even though koalas can trot or gallop, they must also always beware of land predators. The biggest threat is the reddish brown wild Australian dog called the dingo. The small koala is defenseless against this powerful hunter. So koalas must avoid dingoes while traveling on land.

If necessary for an escape, koalas are good swimmers too. But if they smell trouble, they will always climb up the closest tree. That is where they are safest.

Koalas can detect danger by using their excellent senses of smell and hearing.

Being nocturnal, koalas become more active after dark than during daylight. But like children, koalas can't stay up all night. Most people sleep about 8 hours each day. During a typical day, koalas sleep between 18 and 22 hours.

Some people think koalas are lazy because they sleep so much. Or because they seem to move in slow motion. They definitely don't appear to be in a hurry! And there is a very good reason. Eucalyptus leaves are low in nutrients (NU-tree-ents). Even though koalas eat a lot of them, the leaves don't provide them with much energy. So koalas must conserve their energy by moving slowly and getting plenty of sleep.

Sleeping at least 18 hours a day helps koalas conserve energy.

Unlike most mammals, koalas never make dens or permanent homes. They do have home territories, but they will not stay in one particular tree.

Also, koalas like to be alone. Several koalas may live in the same area, but they will not socialize (SO-shul-ize), or hang out together. If more than one ends up in the same tree, they will avoid each other and stay on separate branches.

Koalas spend time with each other only when they are ready to mate or when a mother is raising her baby.

This koala mother is teaching her baby to climb safely.

One male will usually share his home territory of about 15 different trees with up to 6 females.

He will mark his territory by rubbing a scent gland on the center of his chest against the bottoms of his trees. The odor is an invisible message. It warns other males that they are not welcome in his area.

Koalas are usually quiet, but they can be very noisy if they have something to say.

Koalas also communicate by making noises, which include growling, grunting, groaning, and whining. When the males want to attract a mate, they sit on their rumps, lift their snouts skyward, and roar.

Scientists report that the male's courting call sounds more like a ferocious beast than a mild-mannered koala.

Males can begin breeding after they turn 3 years old. Females usually can breed by age 2.

On average, female koalas reproduce about once every other year. They have one baby, called a joey, at a time. Twins are extremely rare. Males and females will always go their separate ways after mating. The female koala raises the baby by herself.

Baby koalas are born pink, bald, blind, and about the size of a jelly bean. A newborn koala must immediately crawl into its mother's pouch. This journey is very difficult and usually takes about 5 minutes.

Once inside the pouch, the joey begins feeding on its mother's milk. Even though the pouch opens upside down, the tiny koala can't fall out. A muscle at the bottom of the pouch tightens to keep the baby inside. While her joey is safe and snug in her pouch, the mother koala can continue life as normal.

This young joey is tightly holding onto its mother's fur.

At around 6 months old, the baby pops its furry face out for its first peek at the world.

The joey now looks like a miniature version of its mother. It communicates to her in high-pitched squeaks.

By this time the joey begins to want more to eat than just milk.

Mother koalas do a good job of protecting their young joeys.

So the mother gives her baby a food called pap, which is partly digested eucalyptus leaves that she has pre-chewed. The baby likes this new food. Pap gives the joey a little taste of eucalyptus and prepares its stomach for digesting solid leaves.

By 8 months old, a joey can pull itself out of the pouch. The joey clings to its mother's belly as she climbs through the trees. If it feels frightened or tired, it can always go back into the pouch. As it grows bigger and braver, the koala baby begins riding piggyback or on top of its mother's head.

By 12 months old, the joey wants to eat only eucalyptus leaves. No more mother's milk and no more pap. The mother koala begins teaching her baby which eucalyptus leaves are good to eat.

At about 18 months, the young koala is now ready to leave its mother and live alone. It will find a territory of its own.

Koalas are not really fully grown until they turn 4 years old. Scientists say koalas in the wild usually live between 10 and 14 years.

Koalas spend most of their life high up in trees, and not much time on the ground.

People of all ages seem to like koalas. Yet humans have been the biggest threat to their survival. There was a time when koalas almost disappeared completely. That was long ago, when people shot them for sport and to sell their coats. Since 1927 Australia has had laws that protect koalas from being killed.

But the places where they live are not protected. Today the major threat to koalas is the loss of their habitat. As cities expand into their eucalyptus forests and replace trees with buildings, many koalas lose their homes. Some koalas have been seen in dangerous traffic areas. And they have been killed by motorists who do not expect them to be there.

The safest place for a young koala is riding piggyback on its mother.

Loss of habitat continues to force koalas into other human environments.

They have been spotted perched on fences and on street signs. They have climbed up telephone poles. These koalas are lost and scared. Fortunately, there are people who are trying to help them.

With our help, koalas will continue to live in their original wild habitats.

186

Many koalas are rescued and taken to parks and preserves. These protected areas are sanctuaries (SANK-chu-air-ees), or safe places, for them to live. Some of these sanctuaries have hospitals that treat injured koalas and then return them to their original habitats. Others provide them with permanent homes.

The koala is a threatened species. Some scientists estimate that there are about 40,000 to 80,000 koalas left in the wild. And although the koala still faces many challenges to its future, the Australian government and people who care about koalas are helping to protect them.

MY WILD ANIMAL ADVENTURES

The date of my adventure: _____

The people who came with me: _____

_____

Where I went: _____

What wild animals I saw:

_____   _____

_____   _____

_____   _____

_____   _____

The date of my adventure: _____

The people who came with me: _____

_____

Where I went: _____

What wild animals I saw:

_____   _____

_____   _____

_____   _____

_____   _____

MY WILD ANIMAL ADVENTURES

The date of my adventure: _____

The people who came with me: _____

_____

Where I went: _____

What wild animals I saw:

_____   _____

_____   _____

_____   _____

_____   _____

The date of my adventure: _____

The people who came with me: _____

_____

Where I went: _____

What wild animals I saw:

_____   _____

_____   _____

_____   _____

_____   _____

MY WILD ANIMAL ADVENTURES

The date of my adventure: _____

The people who came with me: _____

_____

Where I went: _____

What wild animals I saw:

_____   _____

_____   _____

_____   _____

_____   _____

The date of my adventure: _____

The people who came with me: _____

_____

Where I went: _____

What wild animals I saw:

_____   _____

_____   _____

_____   _____

_____   _____

MY WILD ANIMAL ADVENTURES

The date of my adventure: _____

The people who came with me: _____

_____

Where I went: _____

What wild animals I saw:

_____   _____

_____   _____

_____   _____

_____   _____

The date of my adventure: _____

The people who came with me: _____

_____

Where I went: _____

What wild animals I saw:

_____   _____

_____   _____

_____   _____

_____   _____

191

WEB SITES

You can find out more interesting information about Pandas, Cheetahs, Elephants, Koalas, and lots of other wildlife by visiting these web sites.

www.cheetah.org/
Cheetah Conservation Fund

www.discovery.com/
**Discovery Channel
and its programs like
"Animal Planet" and "Discovery Kids"**

www.nwf.org/
National Wildlife Federation

www.panda.org/
**World Wildlife Fund
and its "Just For Kids"**

www.ran.org/intro.html
**Rainforest Action Network
and its "Kids Corner"**